Math Games

MATH GAMES

by Shawn Azami

ISBN: 9798501263673 © 2022

Table of Contents

Table of Contents [cont.]

Introduction

Ages 6-14. New and innovative Math-Based games designed to accelerate children's learning.

"MATH GAMES" is a compilation of fun games with the best feedback from learning centers, daycares, parents, teachers, and kids alike.

Enjoy teaching your kids dozens of **MULTIPLAYER** and **ONE-ON-ONE** games designed to boost their math skills, critical thinking, memory, and more!

Overview

Great for road trips, family gatherings, birthday parties, learning centers, charter schools, daycares, tutoring, babysitting, and more!

These new innovative games will keep the kids busy while they learn.

Adults should play with them at first, then help them move on to friends and siblings.

The learning strategies and memorization develop automatically while the children are having fun, so the games don't feel like schoolwork.

Thank you for inviting my work into your homes and classrooms.

Have fun as you watch them learn!

ADAM UP!

These first simple games will help sharpen our basic math.

Let's start with Adam's game, then we'll add several variations.

Take out all the jokers and face cards from a typical deck of playing cards so you have **ACE through 10 ONLY**.

You will be using this **'numbers-only'** deck for many games to come.

** The ACE will ALWAYS count as a 1 throughout this book for every game. **

Now give every player two cards each.
You have to **<u>ADD UP</u>** your card values.
Whoever ends up with the HIGHEST TOTAL keeps all 4 cards, then play again until the cards run out.

Player with the most cards wins!

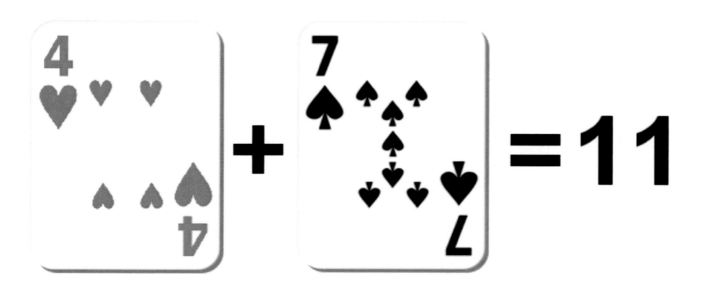

IN CASE OF A TIE:

For a **2-Player** tie, leave all the cards facedown and play again. Whoever wins the next round takes ALL the cards!

With **3 or more Players** and 2 or more winners, distribute the losing cards evenly to the winners.

If the cards cannot be distributed evenly, disregard the odd card and play again.

For example, suppose there was an extremely rare case where 5 players had total card values of: 12, 12, 12, 10, and 9.

The 3 winners can't take the 4 losing cards evenly.

So the winners would simply take one card each, and the remaining card would be taken out of the game.

*Use the same steps above in case of a tie for the next 3 variations.

MINUS MINDY

Again, take out all the face cards so you have the **ACE through 10 deck**, and give every player two cards.

This time, however, you have to **SUBTRACT** your lowest card *from* your highest card.

So in the last game, the order of the cards didn't matter, but now they do.

You want them to make the distinction between adding and subtracting numbers.

Make sure everyone puts their cards in the correct order before they subtract them.

The highest number MUST be FIRST, or they will end up with negative answers.

This time, whoever ends up with the **LOWEST** answer keeps all 4 cards. Again, play until the cards run out.

Player with the most cards wins!

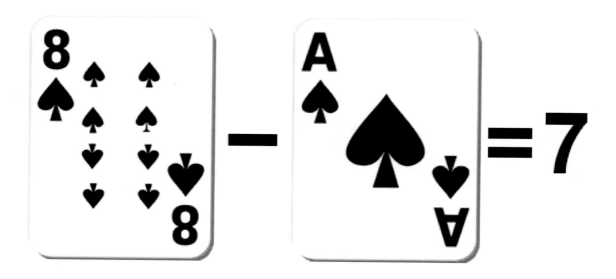

The Ace is always a 1 for every game.

TIMES TRACEY

The final two versions of this game may be a bit advanced for the youngest ones but the earlier you learn your times tables, the better.

Again, make the **ACE through 10 deck**.

This time (as you may have guessed) you have to **<u>MULTIPLY</u>** the card values and the **HIGHEST** answer keeps all 4 cards.

For the younger ones, you can try taking out some of the larger numbers like 7, 8, 9, and 10. Then gradually work your way up to the full Ace through 10 deck.

You can even sneak in the **<u>DIVISION</u>** version when they get cards that can divide evenly, like 10 and 2 or 8 and 4.

Just make sure they put the cards in the correct order, from highest to lowest.

In the division version, since the answer becomes smaller, the **LOWEST** answer keeps all 4 cards.

Your goal is to be able to switch back and forth between ALL FOUR variations every several hands.

Try and work up to every variation!

MATHy Mike

Mike does nothing but math all day. His game uses **ALL 4 Arithmetic Operations**. Add, Subtract, Multiply, and Divide!

To win this game, you need to know your arithmetic really well, like Mathy Mike.

10 PLAYERS MAX.

Make the **ACE through 10 deck once again** by removing the face cards. Now place the deck facedown in the center.

This game goes clockwise with everyone taking turns drawing two cards.

Once you draw two cards, show them to everyone and say any one of the four operations: **"Add"**, **"Subtract"**, **"Multiply" OR "Divide!"**

Whoever says the right answer first gets to keep the cards. Then your turn is over and whoever is to your left is next.

You **CANNOT** answer if you also drew the two cards.

WATCH OUT before you say DIVIDE!

If you say, "DIVIDE", and the card values don't divide evenly...you're OUT!

So you can say, "DIVIDE" if you pick a 10 and a 2, or an 8 and a 4, but not on a 7 and a 3 or a 9 and an 8.

If they do divide evenly, only whole number answers are accepted. So for 8 and 4, the answer 2 is accepted, but NOT 1/2.

Also, if someone says **"SUBTRACT"**, it automatically means the highest card minus the lowest card.

Whoever ends up with the most cards before the deck runs out wins!

Can I play?

MOLLY'S MEMORY

This is a cool math twist from the old familiar "Memory Game".

Just a quick refresher, the Memory Game was when all the cards or pictures were facedown and you had to pick two exact matches in order to keep them.

If you were right and got a match, you would go again until you miss.

Once you miss, it was the next player's turn.

Whoever had the most cards or symbols in the end, won the game.

To play MATH MEMORY, make the same **ACE through 10 deck** and place all the cards facedown in pairs of 2 as shown below. (**You should have 20 pairs**)

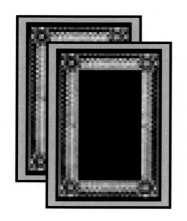 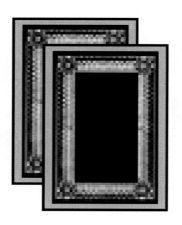 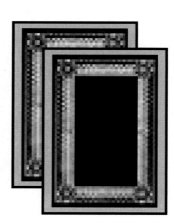

Whoever goes first picks two piles and CANNOT MIX the cards.

You have to **ADD** *OR* **SUBTRACT** the values of each pair of cards.

If the sums **OR** differences match in **ANY** way, you get to keep the cards. If not, you must put them back where they were and it's the next player's turn.

So 10-10 and 2-2 would **MATCH** since each pair subtracts to zero.

5-6 and 8-3 would also match, since each pair adds up to 11.

You can also add one pair and subtract the other as shown below.

Molly's Memory Match: 9-1 = 3+5 = 8

Whoever ends up with the most cards wins!

Sometimes a few pairs may remain in the end that don't match, but that's okay.

The game would end there.

If you like, you can *preset* the piles beforehand to make sure they all match in some way.

For a **Super Challenge**, try adding a third card and see who wins with piles of 3!

Advanced Variation

SALLY'S SUM

Sally can make her cards **add up** to 45 faster than anyone I've ever seen. How does she do it?

This is a **6-PLAYER MAX** game, however, it's played best with four players or less.

Make the **ACE through 10 deck** once more and give every player **1 CARD** each to start with.

Place the deck facedown in the middle so everyone can draw cards.

In this game, and in all future games, you can draw cards to see who goes first, or simply pick someone to go first.

Everyone starts drawing **1 card** at a time in **clockwise** order until they want to **STOP**.

The goal is to make all your cards **add up to 45**, or closest to it, **WITHOUT** going over.

There is NO RESHUFFLING. Once the deck runs out, the game is OVER.

The key in Sally's Sum is **When to Stop** drawing cards.

Remember, if your total is ever higher than 45, your hand is dead and you're out!

You might want to supervise as they draw cards to make sure everyone is adding correctly and not going over.

Once you say "DONE", you can no longer draw cards but make sure and wait until **EVERY PLAYER HAS FINISHED** before turning your cards over.

When every player has finished and no one wants anymore cards, all the hands can be shown in any order.

Whoever has a total closest to 45 or exactly 45, **WITHOUT** going over, wins.

In case of a tie, declare 2 winners or have the winners play again as a form of "Finals".

This game has a great feature in that you can change the difficulty level however you like at any time.

Simply change the desired value from 45 to any other number, higher or lower.

You can even use a clock timer and announce "STOP" at a certain time.

See if anyone figures out Sally's secret...

$$1+2+3+4+5+6+7+8+9 = 45!$$

TAMMY'S TENS

Tammy's Tens is always a favorite with any group, especially when 4 or 5 kids and adults can play at once.

Innovative and fun, this game almost always comes down to the wire, often even to the very last card!

This time, remove all the face cards **AND** the 10s, leaving **Ace through 9** only.

Make three rows faceup with a 10 in the center from the unused cards.

Place all different, **non-matching**, cards around the 10. Which 10 you use and the suits of the cards do not matter.

Just make sure there are **no pairs** and the 10 is in the **center** as shown below:

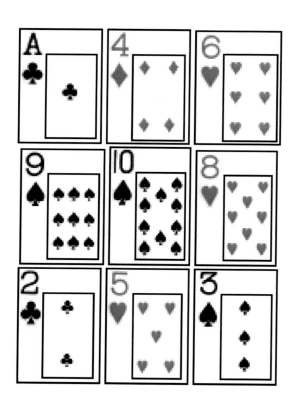

Now, keep the 10 faceup but shuffle the rest of the cards **facedown** and place them around the 10 and shown below.

Tammy's Tens Correct Setup

At this point, you should have **28** cards left from your **Ace through 9** deck.

So for up to 3 players give 8 cards each, 4 players 7 cards each, 5 players 5 cards each, and 6 or 7 players only 4 cards each.

Now, whoever goes first picks any card they like from the facedown cards, and turns it over faceup. Whatever the card is, they must **Subtract** it *from* 10.

So say the card was a 7, then the first answer would be 3, since **10-7 = 3**.

Whoever turns over the card has to see if they have the answer. In this case, if they have a 3 in their hand they can place it over the 7 on the board.

Now the new answer is **10-3 = 7**. So if they have a 7 they can throw it back down over the 3, if not, they say "PASS" and their turn is over.

The next player, always going clockwise, has to do the same thing: check for the answer in their hand and place it over the card on the board, or say "PASS".

If everyone passes all the way around, **the last person that put a card down** gets to pick a new card to turn over faceup. This new card gets subtracted from 10 once again, and reveals a **new answer**. This process continues in clockwise order.

WHOEVER LOSES ALL THEIR CARDS FIRST WINS!

This is a very sweet game that keeps interest and often has a surprise winner.

A unique thing happens when a 5 is turned over and you have more than one 5 in your hand.

Since the new answer remains 5, you can go ahead and place all your 5s down in a row, then you would have to PASS.

Just to make sure you understand the gameplay, the next page shows an example of a game midway through with 4 players.

Each player's turn is explained in order.

The first payer turned over a 3, which you can't see, then placed a 7♣ over it, didn't have a 3, and everyone passed.

The 2nd player turned over the 4♥, didn't have a 6, and everyone passed.

The next player turned over an Ace then put the 9♠ over it, and everyone passed.

The last player turned over an 8, put a 2 over it, then an 8 over that, then the 2♠ over that as you see above, and passed.

Very often in this game, a player or players will be waiting for one specific card to become available for them to win since they will have only 1 card left.

This will create a memory for that specific subtraction that they won't forget.

Played enough times, they will end up never forgetting any of the single-digit subtraction combinations.

Just in case:

In an almost impossible case where:

1. every card gets turned over
2. everyone still has cards left
3. everyone passed all the way around

Declare the winner by whoever has fewer cards in their hand.

In case of a tie, declare multiple winners.

Simply add more 10s in the middle for more advanced variations. Even all four 10s will work. Just place the appropriate amount of cards around them.

You will be forced to have some pairs, or matching cards, but it's okay.

The game still works great as long as you make sure the facedown cards are always Ace through 9 only.

Add more 10s for advanced play!

RACHEL'S ROLLERS

Rachel just started rollerblading. Whenever she goes to practice it feels like she's on a rollercoaster.

This might be the only familiar game in the book, but it's sort of a 'primer' for the next two games.

When everyone takes to this game and starts playing faster and faster, it feels like a rollercoaster.

Make the same **ACE through 10 deck** with no face cards and give everyone **10 cards each** for 4 players or less, and 8 cards each for 5 players.

The rules are very simple and the game moves quickly. Your kids may have already played a version of it.

Everyone goes in clockwise order throwing down **1 card at a time**.

The goal is to place a card down **1 value above OR below** the previous card.

WHOEVER LOSES ALL THEIR CARDS FIRST WINS!

So if you see a 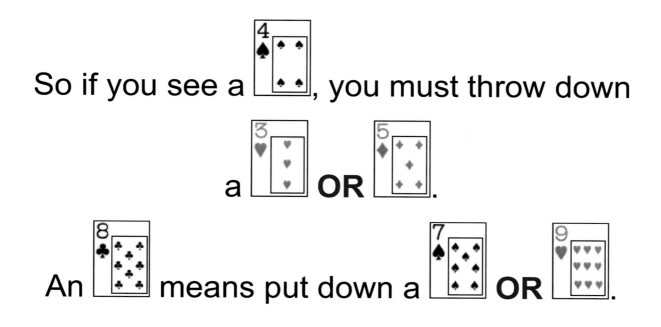, you must throw down

a OR .

An means put down a OR .

WRAPPING AROUND THE 10 AND THE
ACE **IS** ALLOWED!!!

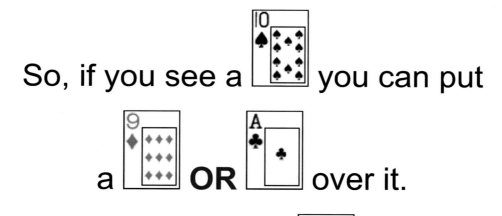

So, if you see a you can put

a OR over it.

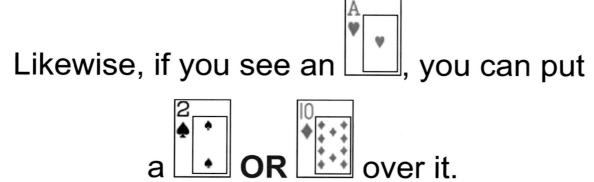

Likewise, if you see an , you can put

a OR over it.

If you don't have a card 1 above or 1 below the previous card, you must say "PASS" and your turn will be skipped.

If everyone says "PASS" all the way around, the **Last Player** that threw down a card goes again. They **RESTART** the round by throwing **ANY** card they like.

Fun Face Card Variation:

I've added a unique variation to spice things up if you have a full cast of 4 or more players.

At the start of the game, give each player 1 additional card: **a face card**.

These Kings, Queens, and Jacks make the gameplay go in reverse, meaning **counterclockwise** and are followed by a 2nd card of your choice but...

You can only use them if you **DON'T** have a card 1 above or 1 below and your ONLY option is to "PASS".

Make sure they use the face cards correctly, you can't just throw them down whenever you want.

Once someone throws down a face card, they get to put down **ANY** 2nd card of their choice over it.

Now going **counterclockwise**, the player to the **RIGHT** goes next, and the rest follow.

The counterclockwise play continues until someone else uses a face card.

If the face card is your last card left, all you have to do is throw it down when it's your turn and you win.

You could still possibly lose, however, if another player went before you with only a face card. So make sure and use it earlier.

See how fast everyone can play without anyone making a mistake!

FRANK'S FISH

Frank likes to fish, and sometimes his cousins come to help. When they catch a big fish together they go crazy. Who will catch the big fish first?

Use a full 52-card deck with **three 10s removed**. I like to keep the 10♠ because ♠♠spades♠♠ look like fish.

This is a **4-PLAYER MAX** game since you have to give each player a King to start.

The King represents you, the fisherman. After you give everyone a King, shuffle the deck with the single 10 and place it facedown in the center of the players.

Frank doesn't like to catch "ODD" fish when he first arrives, so you can only gather "EVEN" cards at first.

Each player draws **1 card at a time**, clockwise. If your card if is even, keep it. If not, discard it into a dead pile facedown.

This ends your turn since you can only keep 1 even card at a time at first. Place your "evens" faceup as you gather them.

If the deck runs out, simply **reshuffle** the discards and resume play.

Matching cards and face cards don't count and are discarded. So if you already have a 4 and draw another 4, you must discard it and your turn is over.

Place the first card you keep halfway on top of your King faceup, and each card after halfway on top of the last, and so on.

Again, if you draw a card you can't use, throw it facedown into a dead pile. It's okay to have the dead pile next to the drawing pile, as long as you don't mix them up.

In **ANY ORDER**, once you finish your "EVEN" fish line, you can then start your "ODD" fish line.

Whoever makes both fish lines first wins.

First: (2, 4, 6, 8) **then** (Ace, 3, 5, 7, 9)

Now, if somewhere down the line you draw a Queen or a Jack that's the **SAME SUIT** as your King, you get to keep them. These are your **COUSINS** coming to help.

Getting a same-suit **cousin** is great because now you get to draw **2 cards at a time,** and you're allowed to catch **2 fish per turn max.** A second cousin allows **3 draws and 3 fish per turn max**!

Frank's Fish Gameplay Sample:

This player *caught* the 6♣, completing his "evens", then the Q♦ allowing him to draw 2 more times, but his turn ended when he drew the 5♥ since that's two "catches".

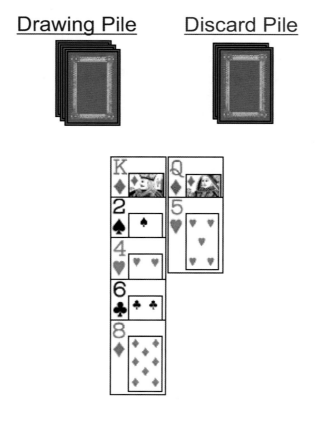

The cousins let you draw more cards, but the fish catching ends your turn.

So in the last example, if the player drew the ♦Jack of Diamonds♦, he could draw 3 more times, **unless he caught a 3rd fish**.

Now what about that single 10♠, or the Big Fish in the deck?

Whoever draws the big fish gets to go home early and automatically wins....but

WAIT! You can only bring in the Big Fish if you have **BOTH** cousins helping you!

So if you draw the 10♠ and don't have a Queen AND a Jack yet, you're going to have to throw it back!

Let's see who can win the fastest, either by making both fish lines first OR by catching the **Big Fish** with **BOTH** cousins!

Remember, throw down ALL matching/paring cards and ALL face cards that don't match your King's suit.

KEVIN'S CONNECTIONS

This game, and all its variations, has been regarded as one of the best 2-Player games by dozens of parents and teachers.

Make the **ACE through 10 deck** except **ADD ANY 2 FACE CARDS.**

Put all 42 cards facedown in 7 rows and 6 columns, as shown below.

(Player 1's First Row)

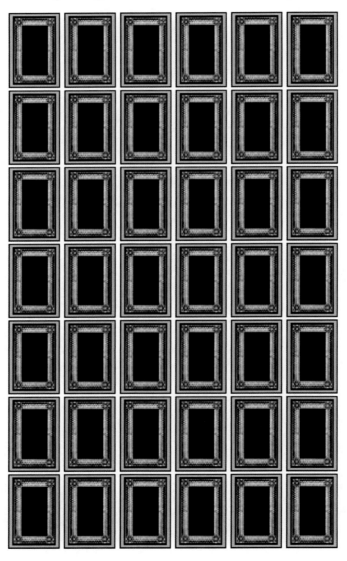

(Player 2's First Row)

This is a **2-PLAYER GAME**, with one player sitting at the top and one player at the bottom, but of course, you can share and play teams.

If desired, every game in this book can be played one-on-one.

The goal is to get to the other side by turning over your cards and connecting them **Even-to-Even** OR **Odd-to-Odd**.

You can go up, down, left, right, diagonal, and even backward, as long as ALL your cards are "connected" in some way.

You start **every round** by turning over a card from your BOTTOM ROW.

If it's 'even', you can move again by selecting another 'even' card that's touching the previous card.

If it's is 'odd', you can keep going only by selecting more 'odd' cards that are touching.

Once you hit a card that doesn't match (odd-to-odd OR even-to-even), then your turn is over and it's the opponent's turn.

Remember, both players must restart **every round** from the beginning, selecting a new card from their own BOTTOM ROW.

You can, however, re-connect or newly-connect to previous cards as long as they match **Even-to-Even** OR **Odd-to-Odd**.

The 2 face cards are *neutral*, meaning you can connect to them and continue.

So if you turn over a 4, then an 8, then hit a King, it would count as an even card.

If your opponent runs into it later with an odd card, it would count as an 'odd', and so on.

You may even win by landing on one.

If by chance you happen to start off on a face card, your next card will dictate whether your path is odd or even.

Let's get a clear visualization of the gameplay and what a winning example looks like.

Winner: Top Player

Here, the **Top Player** went first and picked the **9♦**, then went all the way through without missing selecting all 'odds' (**9♦, 5♥,**

Ace♠, **7♥**, **Queen♦**, **Ace♣**, and **3♦**) until he got to the other side and won.

A win on a single turn is extremely unlikely but I just wanted to show you a clear visual before we move on.

Notice the face card ♦Queen counted as an 'odd' number, allowing the player to continue.

Now if the player's 4th card was 'even', like the **6♦** instead of the **7♥**, he would have had to STOP as shown below.

(Top Player)

(STOP)

His turn would have been over, and he would have had to **restart** from his bottom row next round.

You must ALWAYS restart your turn from your own bottom row.

Now suppose the **Bottom Player** went next from *her* first row and picked the **10♦** then the **4♠**, then the **8♥**, and stopped on the 'odd' **7♠**, as shown below.

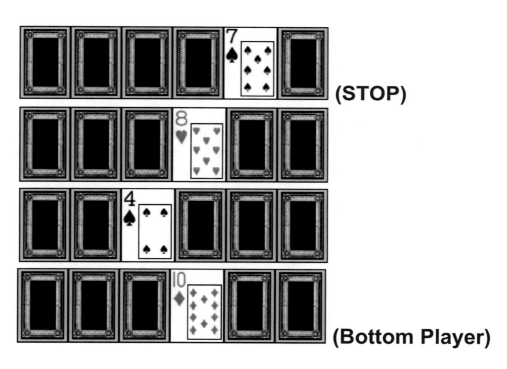

(STOP)

(Bottom Player)

What would the full game look like with both player's cards?

Putting the previous two examples together, we can see how each player turned over 4 cards, then had to stop.

Top Player

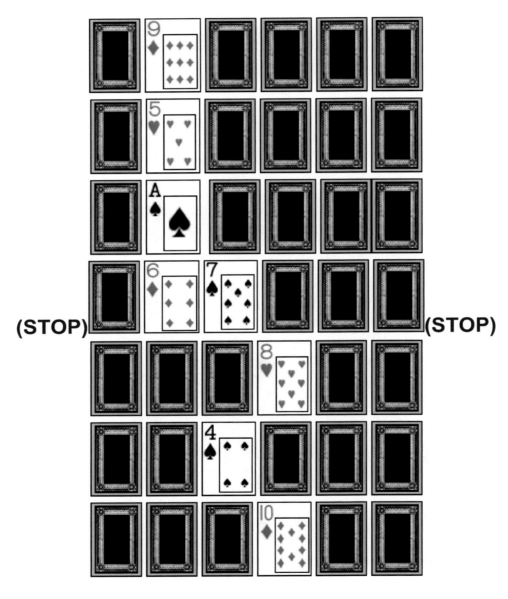

(STOP)   (STOP)

Bottom Player

To win, you need a clear path of **all evens** or **all odds** with or without face cards from your first row up to the last row.

You can connect to your previously turned over cards **OR to your opponent's cards to help you out.**

If you finish your bottom row cards before anyone wins, simply use your **2nd row** cards as your new starting row.

Since the previous example was taken from an actual game, I displayed the final result on the next page so you have a clear visual before you play.

Player 2 won using this path:

(2♣, 4♠, 10♥, 6♦, 8♣, Jack♦, 6♣)

The **blue** arrows to the left of each card on the next page show the player's path to victory from bottom to top.

Previous Example Final Result

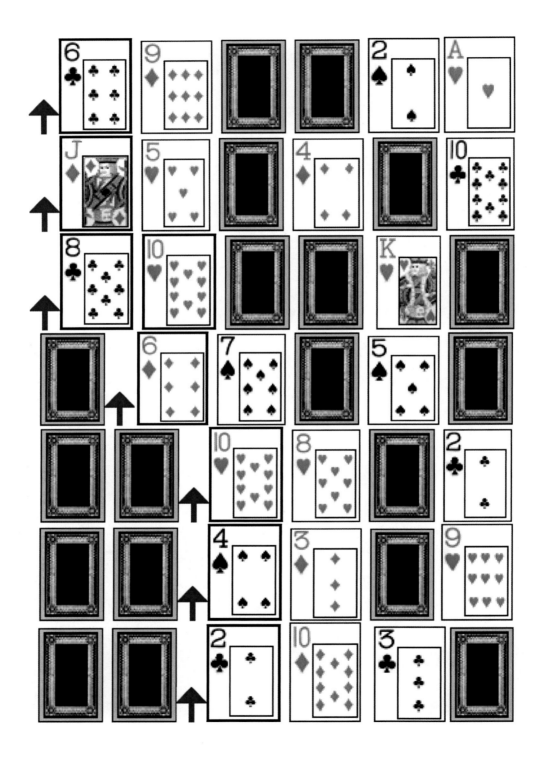

Kevin's Connections

This game has deceptively more strategy than you think.

Where you start and where you connect to can make a big difference.

Being able to know what facedown cards are left by subtracting out the faceup cards can be a big factor as well.

This is another game where you can easily adjust the difficulty level.

You can add or subtract columns to fit younger and older kids accordingly.

One variation I use when I see them take interest is to **not stop** the game once someone reaches the other side.

Instead, I make that **1 POINT**. Since the game keeps going, the bottom rows will keep getting used up.

New bottom rows will make the board shorter and shorter until all the cards are turned over. **Most points wins**!

Chuck's Checkers

Chuck never had a Checkers set, so he made his own version. *Check* it out!

Just like Checkers, this is a **2-PLAYER GAME** except each player has 7 cards instead of game pieces.

Give an **Ace, 2, 3, 4, 5, 6,** and **7** to each player. ALL ♥**HEARTS**♥ to one player and ALL ♠**SPADES**♠ to the other.

Have them place all 7 cards faceup in any order from left to right in 1 long row.

You need 4 more long rows in between each player. The backs of the deck can be used as a 'Checkerboard', but it's much better to draw **6 rows of 7 rectangles** on a large paper for this game.

So you need 42 spots in all. A top row with 7 cards, 4 blank rows in the middle, and a bottom row with 7 cards.

Use the next page as a MODEL to set up Chuck's Checkers correctly.

(Make sure you have plenty of space)

PLAYER 1

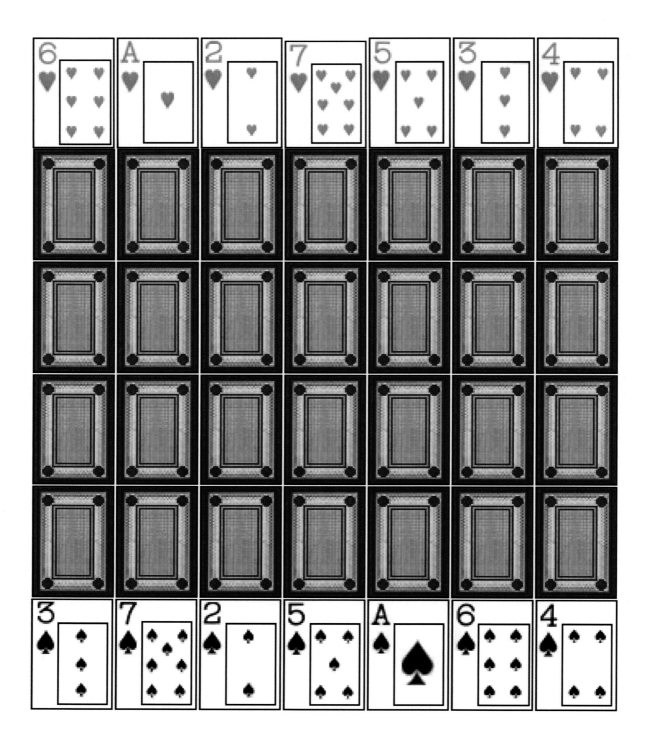

PLAYER 2

49

The goal in conventional Checkers is to capture all your opponent's pieces. In Chuck's Checkers, you have to capture all your opponent's **cards**.

Your 'card-pieces' can move in **ANY** direction. Up, Down, Left, Right, *and* Diagonal.

The value of your cards tell you how many spaces they **MUST** move.

So your Ace can and *MUST* move only 1 square at a time, your 2 MUST move 2 at a time, 3 moves 3, and so on.

This makes the 7 your best card with the farthest range of 7 squares in any direction.

So remember, if you move say a 6, you **HAVE** to make 6 moves with it. Not up to 6, but exactly 6.

Now let's go through the rules on how to play Chuck's Checkers and how to capture cards.

Rule #1 You can ONLY start capturing cards when ALL your cards AND ALL your opponent's cards (all 14 cards) are **OFF** the starting rows.

Rule #2 You CANNOT end your turn on the SAME square you started on.

Rule #3 You CANNOT STOP on the initial starting squares, but you **CAN** PASS THROUGH them during play!

Capture your opponent's cards by '*Hopping*' over them vertically, horizontally, or diagonally, and landing on a **non-occupied** square.

Place captured cards in a discard pile.

Whoever makes the **Final Capture** wins!

The next page shows Chuck's Checkers during play.

How can **PLAYER 2** capture the 3♥ and 5♥ and where can he stop?

♥ PLAYER 1 ♥

♠ PLAYER 2 ♠

From the previous example, **PLAYER 2** can capture his opponent's 5♥ and 3♥ in one turn.

You can acquire multiple captures, just like regular Checkers.

He can move his 4♠ up 1 square, then turn left and "Hop" over the 3♥ and take it. Then he can "Hop" up over the 5♥ and take it before coming down 1 space right where the 5♥ was.

So the initial starting squares are "in play" and part of the board, you just can't STOP on them.

The "Hop" counts as only 1 move. So in total, **PLAYER 2** made 4 legal moves and didn't stop on any initial starting squares.

You can NEVER stop on the square you started on or on the initial starting squares. However, you can **PASS THROUGH** either as often as you like!

PAUL'S PYRAMID

Let's see who can build the best pyramid for Paul and get the most points!

For this game you will use the **ACE through 10 deck,** and it's a **3-PLAYER MAX** game, but usually played 2-player.

Each player receives **13 cards,** all facedown.

Have them make a **FOUR-ROW** pyramid **WITHOUT** looking at the cards.

Use 6 cards on the bottom, then 4 cards, then 2, then 1, as shown below:

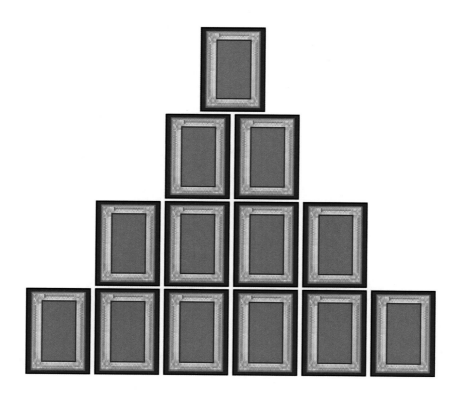

Paul's Pyramid 13-Card Starting Setup

In turn, each player flips over **1 card** at a time until their pyramid is completely revealed, but WATCH OUT...

You have to follow two rules

Rule #1

Once you turn over a card, you **MUST SWITCH CARD POSITIONS** with one of your facedown cards **WITHOUT LOOKING** at the other card. It's locked in after that.

Your last card will be the only card you don't position-switch. You just turn it over on your final turn.

Rule #2

The cards in each row must be added up (left to right) with your HIGHEST TOTAL on the bottom row, 2nd highest in the 2nd row, 3rd highest after that, and your single card at the top must be your lowest total.

Each row total is worth **1 point**

At the end of the game, whoever has the highest bottom row total gets **1 point**, highest 2nd row gets **1 point**, and so on.

So you add up the card values from left to right with the top card being its own total.

Now, if someone's point totals aren't in highest to lowest order, their pyramid crumbles and they get **ZERO POINTS**.

This could happen even before the game is over, so watch out!

Again, your 6-card row must have the highest total, the 4-card row next highest, the 2-card row after that, and the single card the lowest.

If you turn over a high card like a 9 or 10, don't always put it at the top to win the row. It might crumble your pyramid!

Sometimes enough cards are revealed that you realize you can't lose a row, in that case, don't put anymore high cards there.

Low cards like an Ace or a 2 shouldn't always go at the top either, you might lose that row for points.

However, if your pyramid is starting to get full, you might have to place a low card at the top to keep it from crumbling.

Here's an example of a finished pyramid with the totals at the end of each row.

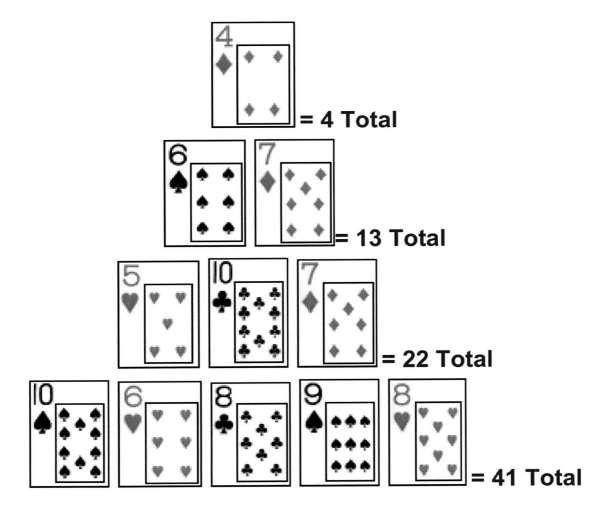

= 4 Total

= 13 Total

= 22 Total

= 41 Total

On your LAST TURN ONLY, your **final card** simply gets turned over and stays where it is.

In case of the obvious tie where a player wins 2 rows and loses the other 2, you can have them play again but with an ODD amount of rows as a form of "tie-breaker".

For more advanced versions, I usually assign **more than 1 point to each row** or take out some of the lowest cards. This will open up as many variations as you like!

Just remember, you **CANNOT** look at the card you are switching positions with, and you **HAVE** to switch **EVERY** card but the final one.

Can I play yet?

EMILY'S 11s

Emily is amazing on the computer. She got a math award for making one of the coolest games you will ever play!

This is a great game in that it brings several math strategies together.

Make the **ACE through 10 deck** once again by removing all the face cards.

This is a **4-PLAYER MAX Game**.

Give each player 10 cards for four players, 13 cards for three players, and 15 cards for one-on-one.

Whoever is chosen to go first simply puts down ANY SINGLE card they like to start the game.

Each player after takes turns putting down **1 card at a time**, always clockwise.

You must make the card or cards on the ground add up to **ELEVEN** by using a **SINGLE** card from your hand.

For example, if someone throws down an 8 and you have a 3, you may pick up the 8 with your 3. (8+3 = 11)

If there is a 6 down and you have a 5, you can put your 5 down and pick up the cards. (6+5 = 11)

Now there could be several cards on the ground like a 3, a 5, and an Ace.

In that case, since 3 + 5 + Ace add up to 9. You can pick them **ALL** up with a 2 in your hand.

Using more than 1 card on the ground to make eleven gives you DOUBLE POINTS!

You receive **2 points** each time you use more than 1 card from the ground, and **1 point** for using a single card.

When you make your packets of eleven, keep them facedown or faceup somewhere off to the side so you know how many points you have.

If you CANNOT make a total of eleven in any way, you **MUST** still **put down 1 card** and it's the next player's turn.

You CANNOT say "pass" and keep your cards, and you CANNOT use more than 1 card at a time to make eleven.

Here is a player's hand after several rounds of play along with the remaining cards on the ground. **What should this player do next?**

Player's Hand after several rounds

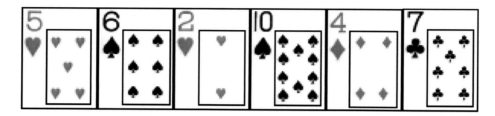

Cards on the ground

 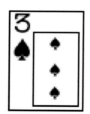 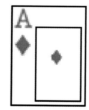

Yes, this player can pick up that Ace♦ with his 10♠, but he should instead pick up the Ace♦ **AND** the 3♠ with his 7♣, since 7+3+1 also add up to 11, giving him **2 points** instead of 1.

When someone puts down their final card, whether they get a point or not, the game is **NOT** over.

The other players continue until *their* final cards are *also* down. There may or may not be cards left on the ground once everyone is finished. Just disregard those cards.

Depending on how many cards they started with and what cards were played, there may be a tie in points between two or more players.

In that case, you have some tie-breaker options.

Whoever had more 2-point packets wins, OR have the winners play again but with fewer cards.

How many strategies are in this game?

Was Emily smart to get a MATH AWARD?

TOM'S TOTAL

Tom has to be very careful when mixing solutions. Great accuracy and efficiency is required. Tom needs an assistant but first wants to see how efficient their math skills are. His game might be tough, but he needs to know who's capable.

This game is my **Personal Favorite** to play with several other players. It tests math skills from different angles, requires patience, and no one has any idea who's going to win!

Your goal is to have **NO CARDS LEFT**, but *how* you lose them will be the key this time.

This is a **5-PLAYER MAX GAME** and uses the familiar **ACE through 10 deck** with no face cards.

Deal out **8 cards** to each player. If you're playing with all 5 players, you should have no cards left.

Again draw or pick a player to go first and everyone follows **clockwise, 1 turn** at a time.

To start the game, the first player must throw down any *SINGLE* **CARD** they like.

The next player must match the **exact value** of that card with **1 or more cards**.

The player after that must now match the **total value** of **ALL** the cards on the ground as does the next player, and so on.

For example, I might go first and throw down an 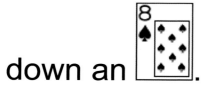.

The next player might throw down a  and a , which equals **8**.

Now, the third player has to exact-match the TOTAL value of ALL the cards she sees.

This would be any combination of cards adding up to 16 because 8♠+2♥+6♦ = 16.

To make a 16, suppose the third player chooses to put down a [10♦] and a [6♣].

Now, whoever goes next has to make a total of 16 + 16, or 32.

If someone **cannot** match the **exact total** of the card values, they must say, "PASS" and it's the next player's turn.

If the game passes all the way around, all the cards in the center are flipped over facedown, and everything RESTARTS.

The **Last Player** to throw cards down gets to RESTART the round by putting down any *SINGLE* CARD.

From here the process continues until someone loses all their cards first and wins.

Let's walk through a game with all 5 players and see how it plays out.

Player One starts and puts down a 3♦.

Player Two needs to match a total of 3 and puts down an Ace♥ and a 2♣.

Player Three sees a total of 6 and puts down a single 6♥.

Player Four now sees a total value of 12, and puts down a 5♠ and a 7♦.

Player Five must now match a total card value of 12+12 = 24 exactly. He happens to have a 10♥, a 10♣, and a 4♠ and puts them all down.

Now back to Player One:
Player One now sees 24+24 or a total of 48, and **CANNOT** make **exactly** 48 in **any** way and says, "PASS".

No one ends up being able to make their cards add up to 48, and everyone ends up saying, "PASS".

Now the game comes back around to **Player Five** who 'RESTARTS' the game since he was the last player to throw cards down.

By 'RESTART', I mean **Player Five** can now throw ANY **single** card he wants.

If it gets passed around to you and you have only 1 card left, you just throw it down and win!

To win Tom's Total, you must be efficient in what cards you select.

For example, if you have to make a 16, you might be able to get rid of more cards than a 10 and a 6. You could use a 7, a 3, a 4, and a 2 instead since **7+3+4+2 = 16**.

This game may go slower than the others, let them take their time. They have to do both the math computations along with the 'most cards to use' computation.

Look over to see if they 'missed one'. Meaning, they may say, "PASS" on a 24 or 32 but *have* cards that add up to those values.

Keep the facedown cards spread clearly so they can see, and **announce** the new totals each time until they get the hang of it.

Hey?

DONNA'S DIAMONDS

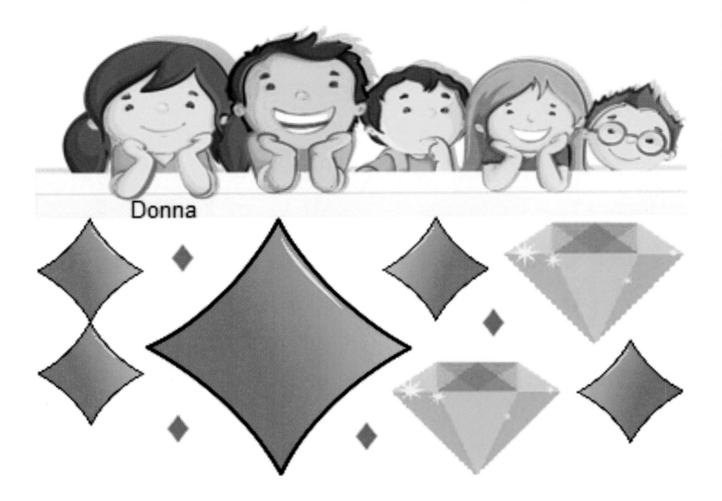

Donna

As far as keeping interest, this game never fails. A great game that makes kids (and most adults) stay busy and want to keep playing.

Take out the face cards and make the **ACE through 10 deck.** Choose how many cards to give to each player.

I like **10** each. That way it takes a while for someone to win, and 4 can play at once.

Your goal is to get RID of ALL YOUR CARDS with the ◆**Diamonds**◆ being the special "Trump" suit.

Everyone goes in clockwise order again, 1 turn at a time.

When you throw cards down, the next player must throw down cards with the **same value or higher,** with the Ace always being a 1.

So if someone throws down a single 5, the next player must throw down a **5 or higher**. If someone throws down a pair like 4-4, the next player must throw down **4-4 or**

higher. If someone throws down triplets like 5-5-5, the next player must throw down **6-6-6 or higher** and so forth. (Ace-Ace is the lowest pair).

You **CANNOT** throw single cards on pairs, or pairs on singles, or triplets over 4-of-a-kind, and so forth.

If you **CANNOT** beat or tie what the last player threw down, you can either say **"PASS"** OR use a **"TRUMP"** card.

Make sure and supervise that everyone is using the Trump cards correctly.

If no one beats your hand and everyone passes back to you, then you get to **RESTART** the round.

By RESTART, I mean you can now throw down ANY card or cards you like.

So if you threw down 8-8 and everyone passed, you can now throw a single 4 in order to get rid of it.

How to use your single ◆Diamond◆ Trump cards:

Say someone throws 9-9 or a single 10, and you can't beat it, you're going to have to make a decision:

Pass **OR** throw a single ◆**DIAMOND**◆. Single Diamonds beat single cards, pairs, triplets, and even four of a kind!

The only thing that beats a single Diamond, is a higher single Diamond. So you **CANNOT** throw down a 7◆ on a 9◆.

Any single Diamond beats any pair or higher.

So can you throw a single 2◆ over even 10-10-10-10? YES!

Only SINGLE Diamonds are Trump cards, NOT pairs with diamonds in them.

WHOEVER LOSES ALL THEIR CARDS FIRST WINS!

If you have some single low cards in the beginning that aren't Diamonds, you should try getting rid of them early before you get stuck with them.

Nothing can beat the 10 of Diamonds, then the 9 Diamonds, then the 8♦, and so on. So having a good **MEMORY** of what diamonds have already been played can be an advantage.

Pairs and triplets with Diamonds in them **DO NOT** count as Trump cards.

Trump cards are **SINGLE CARDS ONLY**.

For example, 7♦-7♠ would still lose to a pair of 7s and above.

There are no "Trump Pairs".

The key in this game is to use your single Diamond cards wisely.

Keep track of them, use them as Trump Cards **OR** as pairs to help you win!

Will's Wallet

Will likes to keep his wallet neat and orderly. He doesn't like loose change or too many bills, but needs enough money for soccer practice and snacks.

Three Versions: **EASY | MEDIUM | HARD**

This is a **5-PLAYER MAX** game.

I like to play with 4, that way everyone can sit evenly around the deck.

Take out all the face cards **AND** the TENS, leaving **Ace through 9 ONLY**.

Place the deck facedown in the center.

Now, give **1 face card** to each player from the unused cards then discard all the other face cards and the tens. They will no longer be used for this game.

Every player must place their face card faceup in front of them.

This face card will act as a **"DECIMAL PLACE"**.

The 3 cards placed to the left of the face card are *dollars*, and the 2 cards placed to the right of the face card are *cents*.

Show the kids some examples before the game starts to get familiar with the decimal place system.

So $826.47 can be represented by an 8♦, a 2♠, a 6♥, any face card, a 4♦, and a 7♣.

Will's Wallet Example Hand = $826.47

Use anything you like for placeholders of the numbered cards if needed.

Everyone takes turns clockwise, drawing **1 card** at a time from the deck.

When you draw a card and want to keep it, you must place it in the **PENNY** spot first on the far right. You must fill up your 5 spots from **RIGHT to LEFT ONLY**.

So here is the order you can teach everyone: 100ths place, 10ths place, 1s place, 10s place, and 100s place.

Now let's go over the rules of Will's Wallet.

RULE #1. If you draw a card you don't want, you **MUST draw the very next card and keep it**. Place it in the appropriate spot and your turn is over.

RULE #2. You must place your cards down **RIGHT to LEFT**: Hundredths, Tenths, Ones, Tens, and Hundreds always LAST.

RULE #3. On rare occasions where the deck runs out before someone finishes filling all 5 wallet spots, they can't win and are OUT!

(SORRY)

Now let's see how to play all 3 versions!

Will's Wallet Easy Version:

In this first simple version, whoever has the MOST money wins!

Ties are very rare, but they both win.

The best someone can have in this version is three 9s on the left and the last 9 and an 8 on the right, or **$999.98**.

So everyone will be throwing down Aces and 2s in hopes to draw higher cards.

Help them out with the specific language of the spots.

For example, the **HUNDREDTHS** place is the 1st spot you fill, but the *HUNDREDS* place is the last spot you fill.

Some may already know dollars, cents, and decimal places but some may not.

With **no zeros** to choose from and being FORCED TO KEEP THE SECOND CARD they draw, they're going to have to make some key decisions in the next 2 versions...

Will's Wallet Medium Version:

Let's make Will's Wallet a little cleaner.

Remember, Will doesn't like loose change. Who can have the most money, but also have the **least amount of coins**?

Since there are 2 ways to win this time, there will often be two different winners.

For example, one player could have **$889.54** for the most money, while another player could have **$276.35** for the least amount of coins (1 dime and 1 quarter).

Someone could even win both sides by making a perfect hand, 999 dollars with a single quarter since there are **NO ZEROS**.

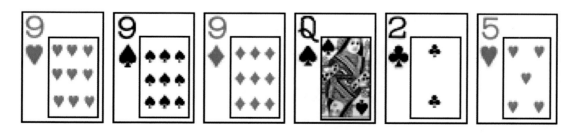

(Medium Version Perfect Hand Example)

Will's Wallet Hard Version:

Will's friend Al has come to play. He says he can make a '**Perfect**' wallet for Will.

Least amount of coins, **AND** least amount of **BILLS,** plus enough to pay for Will's soccer practice and snacks.

So how can you get the least amount of bills and coins with the highest value?

Try playing a few rounds and see what they do.

You might have to remind them of the 50-dollar bill.

With a **$100** bill, a **$50** bill, and a **$5** bill on the left, and a single quarter on the right, the answer to the **Hard Version** becomes...

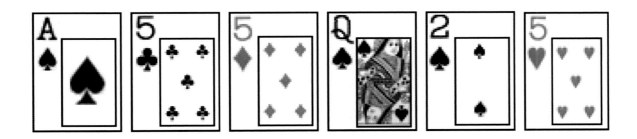

One hundred and fifty-five dollars and twenty-five cents. Three bills and 1 coin.

Remember, there are NO ZEROS and you have to fill every spot.

So you can't use three hundred-dollar bills to make **$300** or use two quarters to make 50 cents.

All 3 variations of Will's Wallet are great for both introducing and practicing dollars and cents without resembling schoolwork.

This new concept of using the face card as a decimal can do wonders!

SAM'S SUITS

Sam likes to wear a lot of different suits, like 4 a week. Let's see who can make the best **6-piece suit** for him in our final game!

<u>**Three Versions:**</u> **EASY | MEDIUM | HARD**

This is a **4-PLAYER MAX GAME** since there are only 4 different card suits.

Remove all the face cards and make the familiar **ACE through 10 deck** one last time, and give each player **6 cards**.

Shuffle the deck and place it in the middle of the players.

Sam's Suits Easy Version:

The FIRST GOAL in the easy version is to simply make all **6 cards the same suit**.

You need to end up with ALL ♠Spades, ♥Hearts, ♦Diamonds, or ♣Clubs.

Your SECOND GOAL is to **ADD UP** the card values.

After receiving the initial 6 cards, the players take turns throwing down and picking up cards **clockwise**, trying to end up with 6 matching suits.

On each turn you can choose **1, 2, or 3 cards at a time** to pick up.

Next you must throw down the SAME number of cards you picked up into a separate discard pile facedown. So you will always have **6 cards remaining** at the end of each turn.

Again, it's okay to place the discard pile next to the drawing pile as long as you don't mix them up.

Once someone finishes, make sure they **DO NOT** show their hand right away.

The game ends only when a *SECOND* **PLAYER FINISHES**.

Finishing 1st gives you **1 extra point**, but ONLY if playing **one-on-one**.

If and when the cards run out before 2 players finish, just reshuffle **BOTH** piles, and start with a fresh single pile facedown again.

When the first 2 players finish and reveal their hands, it's time to **ADD UP** each player's cards + 1 bonus point if needed.

Whoever has the HIGHEST 6-card TOTAL wins, and makes the best and most expensive SAM'S SUIT!

Player 1 | Easy Version

3+8+2+5+10+6 = <u>34</u> (Winner)

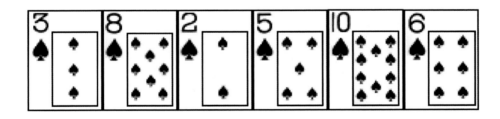

VS.

Player 2 | Easy Version

5+9+1+7+3+4+1 = <u>29</u>

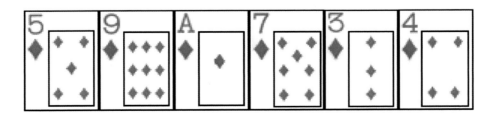

If someone else is picking up hearts and you don't have that many in your hand, or have only small ones, you better switch suits before it's too late!

Make sure and supervise this game at first. Have them keep in mind what suits the others are picking up.

Sam's Suits Medium Version:

In this second version, you still have to get 6 cards to be the same suit and add up the values, except this time there is a very tough twist.

Your **highest 2 cards** have to **Add Up** to the rest of your cards!

For example, you may have an 8♥ and a 10♥ as your highest two cards with a 2♥, 3♥, 6♥, and 7♥ for the rest of your cards.

This would work and follow BOTH RULES.

Since 10+8 = 18, AND 2+3+6+7 also equals 18, the hand below would be VERY good, making 36 points.

Finished Example Medium Version

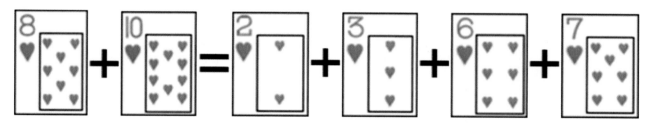

Total Points = (8+10) X 2 = 36

If you were playing **one-on-one** and finished 1st with this hand, you would get the bonus point too, making 37 points!

Again, keep going until **2 PLAYERS** finish and reshuffle if needed.

If there happens to be a tie in any version, have the two winners play again but with 1 less card each.

On extremely rare occasions where ties persist, simply continue the card removal process and a winner will emerge.

Sam's Suits Hard Version:

Al has come to play again. He says he's got the record in the previous **Medium Version**.

Sam's record is 37 points including a bonus point like the last example, but Al says he can beat it!

Can anyone get more than 37 points and still have their **highest 2 cards** add up to the rest of their cards?

THANK YOU

About the Author

Shawn Azami

Shawn grew up in Fresno, California excelling in mathematics in school, taking Calculus as a high school Junior and Calculus II as a Senior. At 18, Shawn was accepted to Cal Poly San Luis Obispo, where he earned degrees in Electrical Engineering Mathematics, and Philosophy.

Always active in sports as a teenager and young adult, Shawn wrestled and played soccer. Currently, he enjoys playing squash and racquetball and is a USTA tennis member.

MATH GAMES" slowly emerged as Shawn designed games to help younger children learn math and critical thinking early, both in his own family and in learning centers and schools.

After several years of great results and numerous suggestions, Shawn combined all the best games into an innovative book with great examples and wonderful illustrations.

Currently living in Fresno, California, Shawn teaches math, and designs and runs his own website:

www.FresnoMathTutoring.com

Also check out...

Learn ABC & My Alphabet
by **Shawn Azami**

Available on AMAZON NOW!

Learn ABCs and character names with **52 Amazing Illustrations** per book!

Ages 3-6

Image Acknowledgments

All graphics not acknowledged were created by the author.

Page (1)
Image link: https://publicdomainvectors.org/en/free-clipart/Mathematics-study/42286.html

Page (2)
Image link: https://publicdomainvectors.org/en/free-clipart/Four-of-hearts-vector-illustration/11016.html
Image link: https://publicdomainvectors.org/en/free-clipart/Seven-of-spades-playing-card-vector-illustration/11236.html

Page (4)
Image link: https://publicdomainvectors.org/en/free-clipart/Dancing-girls/74960.html

Page (5)
Image link: https://publicdomainvectors.org/en/free-clipart/Eight-of-spades-playing-card-vector-drawing/11235.html
Image link: https://publicdomainvectors.org/en/free-clipart/Ace-of-spades-playing-card-vector-image/11232.html

Page (6)
Image link: https://publicdomainvectors.org/en/free-clipart/Vector-clip-art-of-kids-in-front-of-a-blackboard/18502.html

Page (8)
Image link: https://publicdomainvectors.org/en/free-clipart/Cartoon-nerd/40911.html

Page (10, 59, 71) (I'm the cat you never let play, I will be heard!)
Image link: https://publicdomainvectors.org/en/free-clipart/White-cat/76968.html

Page (11)
Image link: https://publicdomainvectors.org/en/free-clipart/Comic-girl-presenting-vector-illustration/16570.html

Page (13)
Image link: https://publicdomainvectors.org/en/free-clipart/Nine-of-spades-playing-card-vector-graphics/11234.html
Image link: https://publicdomainvectors.org/en/free-clipart/Ace-of-spades-playing-card-vector-image/11232.html
Image link: https://publicdomainvectors.org/en/free-clipart/Three-of-spades-playing-card-vector-drawing/11240.html
Image link: https://publicdomainvectors.org/en/free-clipart/Five-of-spades-playing-card-vector-clip-art/11238.html

Page (14)
Image link: https://publicdomainvectors.org/en/free-clipart/Professor-in-green-suit/82556.html

Page (15)
Image link: https://publicdomainvectors.org/en/free-clipart/Lady-farmer/72143.html

Page (18)
Image link: https://publicdomainvectors.org/en/free-clipart/Student-teaching/41428.html

Page (26)
Image link: https://publicdomainvectors.org/en/free-clipart/Vector-illustration-of-rollerblader-cartoon/4288.html

Page (31)
Image link: https://publicdomainvectors.org/en/free-clipart/Glossy-black-fish-vector-illustration/19603.html
Image link: https://publicdomainvectors.org/en/free-clipart/Black-fish-with-mustache-vector-image/19589.html
Image link: https://publicdomainvectors.org/en/free-clipart/Fishing-image/61299.html

Page (35)
Image link: https://publicdomainvectors.org/en/free-clipart/Black-fish-with-mustache-vector-image/19589.html

Page (36)
Image link: https://publicdomainvectors.org/en/free-clipart/Guy-with-spectacles/64450.html

Page (47)
Image link: https://publicdomainvectors.org/en/free-clipart/Hiking-man-vector-drawing/12310.html

Image Acknowledgments

All graphics not acknowledged were created by the author.

Page (54)
Image link: https://publicdomainvectors.org/en/free-clipart/Vector-clip-art-of-twin-brothers-children/18478.html

Page (60)
Image link: https://publicdomainvectors.org/en/free-clipart/Nerdy-girl-with-laptop/73126.html

Page (65)
Image link: https://publicdomainvectors.org/en/free-clipart/Young-scientist/75231.html

Page (72)
Image link: https://publicdomainvectors.org/en/free-clipart/Kids-with-notepaper/80779.html

Page (77,83)
Image link: https://publicdomainvectors.org/en/free-clipart/Vector-illustration-of-cartoon-soccer-player/7884.html

Page (83, 91)
Image link: https://www.pinterest.com/pin/566890671826602205/?autologin=true

Page (85, 91)
Image link: https://publicdomainvectors.org/en/free-clipart/Kid-with-blue-hair/76105.html

Page (95 + inside cover)
Image link: https://publicdomainvectors.org/en/free-clipart/Four-kids-and-circle/65805.html
Image link: https://publicdomainvectors.org/en/free-clipart/Boy-Thinking-of-Question/70001.html

Page (Cover + back cover artwork + page i Math pic)
n1n2 Solutions Santa Rosa, CA 95045, ed@n1n2.solutions

MATH GAMES

by Shawn Azami